In a Land Not Near or Far

Vanessa Zone

BookLeaf Publishing

In a Land Not Near or Far © 2023 Vanessa Zone

All rights reserved.

No part of this publication may be reproduced, stored in a retrieval system, or transmitted, in any form or by any means, electronic, mechanical, photocopying, recording or otherwise, without the prior written permission of the presenters.

Vanessa Zone asserts the moral right to be identified as author of this work.

Presentation by *BookLeaf Publishing*

Web: www.bookleafpub.com

E-mail: info@bookleafpub.com

ISBN:

First edition 2023

*Dedicated to Benjamin. Thank you for helping
me to see the world in new ways.*

The Wish

Once upon a time
In a land not near or far
There lived a little boy
Who wished upon a star
He didn't wish for money
And he didn't wish for toys
But for a better world
For little girls and boys
He wished for clearer skies
And he wished for cleaner seas
He wished for more kindness
And he wished we'd all be free
To be loved and accepted
For who we're meant to be
He blew the star a kiss
And then he went to bed
Images of happiness were dancing in his head
But when the morning came and the boy stepped
outside
He was disappointed
Because much to his surprise
It seemed nothing had changed
How could this be?
Then the boy had a thought
He said "oh....I see"

"If I want to see my wish come true.... it all begins with me!"

Zombie Sue

Let me introduce you to little Zombie Sue
She hasn't any friends at all and she doesn't
know what to do
She's tried quietly joining in on a game of hide
and seek
But it makes poor Zombie Sue's ears hurt when
the children run and shriek!
She's tried to invite the kids to a friendly game
of chess
But for whatever reason this caused them much
distress
She tried to jump on in the pool for a little swim
This only caused the kids to go running home
again
Now poor Zombie Sue was sitting sadly by the
tree
Wondering to herself "why won't anyone play
with me?"
Suddenly...she heard a voice say
"Hi. I'm Timothy and if you'd like to you can
play with me"
Then little Zombie Sue was filled with so much
Joy!
She jumped straight up and ran right over
And ate that little boy!
Oops....

Along The Way

We found a treasure map and
We packed a little snack
We brought along a shovel and
We brought along a sack....
it was just perfect for putting coins inside
We spent the whole day searching
Hopeful we would find
a treasure box of riches
Necklaces and gold
Jewels and trinkets
and secrets very old
Along the way
We found a river ...
that was perfect for splashing
We told jokes ...
perfect for laughing
We found logs ...
perfect for sitting
We found dirt ...
perfect for digging
We never did find the treasure box that day
But I think that just maybe ...
we found some good
along the way

Lucky Penny

5

I found a lucky penny
waiting on the ground for me!
But my dad said it was dirty
and that I should leave it be
Now I guess I'll NEVER have any luck
Poor unlucky me!

Leprechaun

I tried to catch the Leprechaun
I made traps for every room
I set them up so carefully
I added rainbows, flowers and balloons
There were slides and welcome signs
my traps were quite tricky
I even used double sided tape
To make the floor of one trap sticky
I didn't catch the leprechaun
But he was here
Its true.....
I know this for a fact because
He left behind one shoe!

Days

There are good days
And bad days
Silly days
And sad days
There are sunny days
And cloudy days
Smiley days
And pouty days
And sometimes
There are all together yucky days
But if you have a friend who is there to see you
through
They are all really really lucky days

The Big Blue Dragon

There is a big blue dragon
Living way up in the hills
He never hurt a single soul
And he never will
He loves to munch on berries
And to watch the butterflies
He loves to soar above the clouds
In the bright blue skies
So if you ever see the dragon
while he's frolicking about
you needn't cause him any harm
Please don't scream or shout
Just give a little wave and
Continue on your way
And let the big blue dragon
Carry on with his day

The Spider

I called my mom
To tell her there's a spider in my room
She didn't bring a shoe
And she didn't bring a broom
Instead
She brought a cup and
She gently scooped it up
She placed the spider in the yard
It really wasn't very hard
And I'm sure the spider's grateful

Unicorn

Deep in the forest there lives a unicorn
She has a lovely, flowing mane
And a rainbow horn
She loves to frolic in the grass
She loves to munch on leaves
She loves to swim in the cool, clear pond
She loves to nap among the trees
If you are so lucky
To see the unicorn one day
Watch her for a moment
and then be on your way
You see wild things are beautiful
And precious as can be
They should be admired
But can't be owned by
You or me

Your Best

Some days doing your best means you win the
game
Some days you score lots of goals
Some days you get the good grades
Some days it means when things are tough you
still give it a try
Some days it means you get back up even if you
cry
Sometimes it means finding the courage to start
something new
If you're doing your best today
Just know I'm proud of you

World Changer

12

Move the worms from the sidewalk
Kindly hold open the door
Really listen when a friend talks
Pick the trash up off the floor
Compliment a stranger
Send a letter just because
These are the little things
That a world changer does

The Beach

13

Dancing in the waves
Sandy toes
Exploring the caves
Sun kissed nose
Ocean spray
Smiling face
Beach day
Happy place

Pirate's Life

If I were a pirate
I would have a massive ship
It would glide upon the waves
I'd have iced tea that I would sip
I'd hide my treasure in the caves
I would bask in the sun
I'd swim in the sea
And when the day was done
I would look up at the stars
And I would slowly strum
away on my guitar
I'd fall asleep at night
Drifting safely on the sea
And I would say to myself
"This pirate's life is right for me!"

Your Voice

Your voice is important
Your voice can do so much
It can bring about a change
It can lift a person up
It can share a big idea
It's ok to take up space
By using your important voice
To make the world a better place

Silly

I woke up feeling silly
I really don't know why
But I guess I'd rather want to laugh
Than to feel I need to cry
I woke up feeling silly
It's just how I'm going to be
Nothing's going to change it
So come be silly with me

Robot

If I had a robot
I would teach him lots of tricks
I would show him how to dance
He would learn karate kicks
He would cook me up some pancakes
And he'd bring me orange juice too
He would serve delish milkshakes
He would put away my shoes
He would help me with my homework
He would tell me funny jokes
He would help me do the dishes
He would fix things if they broke
My robot would be awesome
The very best ever
If I had a Robot I think I'd name him Trevor

Nature

Admiring trees
and flowers
Watching butterflies
and bees
Climbing up a mountain
or sitting
By the sea
Out in nature
is the place for me

How To Be A Friend

Some friends are good at listening
Some friends love to share
Some friends bake you cookies
Just to show they care
There are friends you see almost every day
And some you see once a year
There are friends who write you letters
And wish they could be near
There are lots of ways to be a friend
So many wonderful things they do
If you are a friend of mine
I want to say "Thank You"

Mistakes

Everybody makes mistakes
This is a simple fact
sometimes a dropped cup breaks
sometimes it stays intact
Either way we always try
our best to make things right
These things help us learn and grow
Mistakes are part of life

Kindness

21

They say kindness is contagious
I hope that this is true
Our world could surely use some more
It may be up to me and you

To My Little Boy

I hope that you stay confident
Don't let anyone dull your shine
Keep doing amazing things
I'm so proud that you are mine

www.ingramcontent.com/pod-product-compliance
Lightning Source LLC
LaVergne TN
LVHW050301200726
843509LV00015B/3094